# Contents

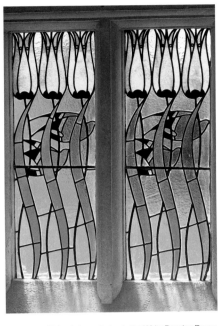

**Above:**  Stained glass window in the White Drawing Room

**Cover:**  The White Drawing Room
© Clive Boursnell 2010

Blackwell, The Arts & Crafts House
Bowness-on-Windermere
Cumbria LA23 3JT
T 015394 46139
E info@blackwell.org.uk
www.blackwell.org.uk

ISBN No. 978-1-906043-06-3

# The Re-awakening

Blackwell was designed in 1898 by Mackay Hugh Baillie Scott (1865-1945), and is one of his largest and most important surviving buildings in this country. The Lakeland Arts Trust purchased Blackwell in February 1999 so that it could be rescued, restored and opened for the public to enjoy. Altogether, the project took four and a half years and cost almost £3,500,000. Blackwell opened on the 4 July 2001 and the restoration overseen by Allies and Morrison architects won two prestigious architecture awards, from the Royal Institute of British Architects and The Civic Trust.

Baillie Scott was an important figure in the development of European domestic architecture, designing Arts & Crafts buildings, furniture and furnishings. The Arts & Crafts Movement, a reaction against the increasing dominance of mechanisation brought about by the Industrial Revolution, was championed by John Ruskin (1819-1900) and William Morris (1834-1896), the 'fathers' of the movement, who sought to re-establish the importance and worth of designer-craftsmen. They advocated a simpler life, in which the home would be a place of harmony and beauty. In line with this ethos, Arts & Crafts architecture was distinguishable from mainstream architecture by hallmarks such as the use of local materials, reference to regional building methods and the employment of local craftsmen.

Blackwell was designed at a key moment, as architects in Britain and Europe began to look afresh at how houses functioned and the way people lived in the home. The twentieth century saw many changes in domestic arrangements and the family unit. Large houses moved away from employing servants and installed modern conveniences such as electrical appliances and en-suite bathrooms. Most houses have been altered to accommodate these changes; it is therefore all the more remarkable, and rare for a house of this period, that Blackwell has largely escaped any alterations and that almost all of its original decorative features have survived.

Blackwell, which was completed in 1901 for Sir Edward Holt, is regarded as a pivotal building for Baillie Scott and was his largest commission during the early phase of his career. It represented a major opportunity to realise many of his ideas which, up until then, he had largely produced as concepts in watercolours and drawings. What makes Blackwell particularly special is that it was designed as a holiday home rather than a

'It is at the fireside that the interest of the room is focused, and in our inconstant climate we may be driven, at almost any season of the year, to seek there that brightness and warmth which we fail to find in the outside world.'

M H Baillie Scott, *The Studio,* 15 November 1895

**Above:** William de Morgan, *Daisy* tile, 1890s, first floor bedroom

Stained glass window, Dinning Room

**Opposite:** Inglenook fireplace with original *Anemone* tiles by William de Morgan, Oliver Thompson Gallery

main residence. The design, therefore, was not restricted by many of the domestic necessities most large houses required. This commission from a wealthy patron really did give Baillie Scott the opportunity to show what he could do, and all of this in a beautiful setting in the heart of the Lake District.

As soon as the Lakeland Arts Trust acquired Blackwell, research was started to investigate how it would have looked originally. Various photographs of Blackwell are included in Baillie Scott's book, *Houses and Gardens*, published in 1906, although there is very little other photographic evidence. Paint scrapes were taken and analysed to discover the original decorative schemes, and a great deal of other detective work was undertaken by a team of historic building specialists. Many of the original features, such as the William de Morgan tiled fireplaces, had simply been boarded up, and most of the beautiful oak floors were laid over with utilitarian carpet tiles. There were original examples of practically every decorative and functional element, and where some were missing, such as the leaf-shaped door handles, replicas were made by a local blacksmith.

When the Trust purchased Blackwell none of the original contents remained; however, from the early photographs we can see that the Holts did not follow whole-heartedly their architect's ideals in respect of furnishing. Much of what they brought to Blackwell appears to be fashionable Regency or Victorian furniture, likely to be made from mahogany or rosewood rather than oak, the preferred timber of Arts & Crafts designers. A photograph of the Main Hall even shows it furnished complete with hunting trophies! Luckily, many designs for interiors by Baillie Scott were published, and it is these, along with his ideas on how to furnish the home in *Houses & Gardens*, that the Trust used to inform the way it has furnished the period rooms. He favoured a deliberate, and rather lean, arrangement of early furniture alongside Arts & Crafts pieces and, following these principles, the Trust has furnished the principal rooms with seventeenth and eighteenth-century oak pieces from the Trust's collection alongside Arts & Crafts furniture and objects.

In common with other Arts & Crafts architects, Baillie Scott sometimes incorporated elements from earlier periods into his designs for houses. This 'recycling' of materials was a way of showing respect for the past by salvaging material that had little monetary value but represented the skill and vitality of craftsmen of earlier times. At Blackwell, Baillie Scott incorporated the eighteenth century fire back in the Dining Room and the paneling in the Main Hall that was reclaimed from St Mary's Church, Warwick.

'...Blackwell is a building of international significance as well as the masterpiece of rare imagination and subtlety.'

Gavin Stamp, *Crafts Magazine*

# A Grand Holiday Home

Blackwell was built as a rural holiday retreat for the Manchester brewery owner, Sir Edward Holt (1849-1928), his wife Elizabeth and their five children. A wealthy industrialist, Holt was active in local government and had the honour of being Lord Mayor of Manchester for two consecutive years, 1907-09. Sir Edward, who was made a baronet in 1916, worked for numerous good causes, helping to improve libraries and Manchester's water supply and sewage works.

Holt's most memorable charity work was in the foundation of the Manchester and District Radium Institute, later known as the Holt Radium Institute and Christie's Hospital. Other charitable works included providing holidays at Blackwell for orphans from the Jubilee School for Girls who had little experience of the countryside, having been brought up in Manchester's slums.

Before the railway line was opened to Windermere in 1847, Bowness was only a small village. The railway brought growing numbers of tourists, who were lured to the Lake District by the romantic scenery, boating on the lakes, and associations with Wordsworth and Ruskin. Many northern industrialists also sought second homes here. The end of the nineteenth century saw a huge boom in large-scale house building in the Lake District, particularly along the eastern shores of Lake Windermere.

Holt bought the land for Blackwell from the Storrs Estate and chose the site for its beautiful setting and prominent location. Sir Edward Holt was Chairman of the Manchester Corporation Waterworks Committee and led the development of the reservoir at Thirlmere, near Keswick, which was completed in 1894. This subsequently led him to recommend the acquisition of the Haweswater Estate, where construction of the dam for another large reservoir started in 1929. These developments were to revolutionise the supply of fresh water to the suburbs of Manchester. Blackwell provided Holt with the perfect Lake District base from which to monitor their progress. He also took an active interest in the local community and became a Justice of the Peace for Windermere in 1907.

Little is known about the craftsmen who worked on the construction of Blackwell as most of Baillie Scott's records were destroyed in two fires later in his career. Sir Edward Holt commissioned Simpsons of

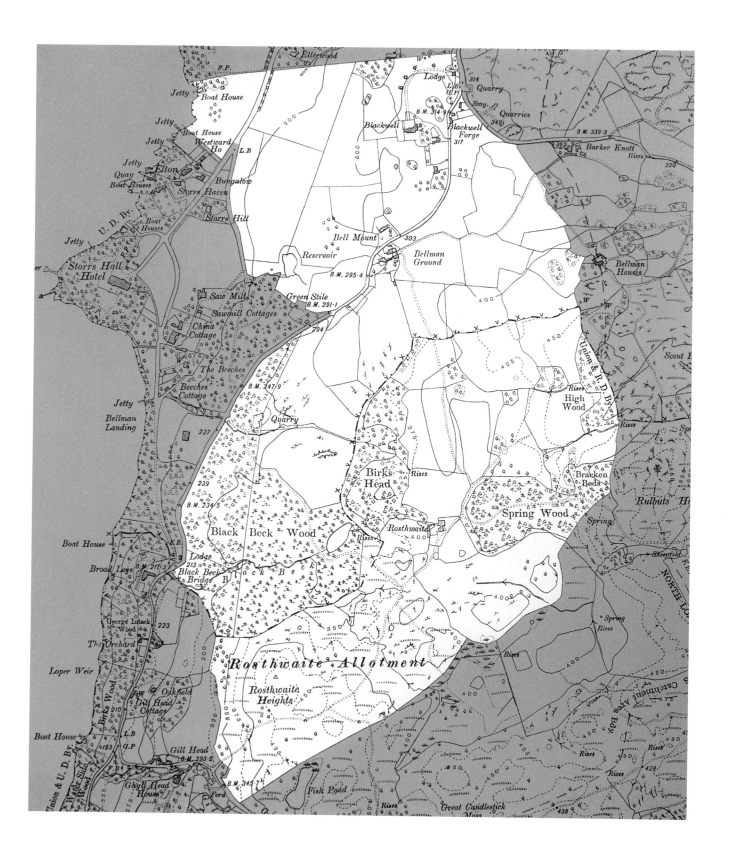

8

Kendal to work on the carving and panelling in the interiors at Blackwell, having first visited Arthur W Simpson in 1894. Arthur Simpson and his son, Hubert, ran 'The Handicrafts', creating fine Arts & Crafts wood carvings and furniture, much of which can still be found in Lake District and Lancashire churches and homes. Their workshop, which opened in 1895, flourished for many years; after Arthur Simpson's death in 1922 his son Hubert ran the company until its closure in 1952. The company was also commissioned to produce carvings for St Margaret's Church in Prestwich, where the Holt family had their main residence.

The Holts visited Blackwell regularly in the first years of the twentieth century. Joseph Holt, the eldest son, was a keen oarsman and also enjoyed racing a 22-foot yacht, the Ibis, which is listed in the Windermere Yacht Club records of 1904. The house design included a boathouse (now privately owned) on the lake where they kept their steam launch S L Wasp, which was very similar to S L Osprey in the Lakeland Arts Trust's collection at the Windermere Steamboat Museum. The Holt's happy period of leisured living was to be cut short with the outbreak of the First World War in 1914. Joseph, their eldest son was killed aged 33 at Gallipoli in 1915. After this the family visited Blackwell less and less frequently. Sir Edward Holt died in 1928 and Blackwell was inherited by his second son, also Edward, who decided to lease it out.

# The Architect - M H Baillie Scott

Mackay Hugh Baillie Scott was born at Beards Hill, St Peter's, near Ramsgate, Kent on the 23 October 1865. He was the eldest of 14 children. His father, also Mackay Hugh Baillie Scott, was a wealthy farmer who owned a large estate in Scotland, as well as a valuable sheep ranch in Australia.

Baillie Scott's architectural career was to span from the 1890s well into the twentieth century. He rose to prominence during the transitional period between the Victorian and Edwardian eras, at a time when society and industry were changing rapidly. Having trained at agricultural college in Cirencester, Baillie Scott was originally destined to take over the management of his father's sheep farm in Australia. However, in 1886 he chose to study architecture instead. From an early age he had shown an interest in nature and the arts, and he spent much of his time sketching the landscape where he grew up, particularly the old country farmhouses and churches. This love of nature and art was to become the foundation of his design philosophy.

In 1886 Baillie Scott was articled to Major Charles E Davis, the City Architect of Bath. It was perhaps not the best practice in which to serve his apprenticeship, as Davis's architecture was in the High Victorian style and offered few opportunities or indeed challenges, for the young and ambitious Baillie Scott.

The city of Bath, however, did provide some inspiration in its many Roman excavations. The marble tiled floors, which can be seen in the entrance porch and in the fireplace in the White Drawing Room at Blackwell, are reminiscent of Roman mosaics, although it is more likely that they were inspired by the Italian Cosmati floors of the eleventh and twelfth centuries.

In 1889 Baillie Scott moved to the Isle of Man after the honeymoon trip he made there with his wife Florence. Initially he worked for the surveyor, Fred Saunderson, in Douglas. Being somewhat removed from mainland influences, he was able to develop his own architectural style, as can be seen by the houses he built there, having set up his own practice in 1892. These include Red House, which he designed for himself and his family, and which showed considerable innovation in planning. He also designed the Majestic Hotel, which was demolished in 2000, and the Castletown Police House.

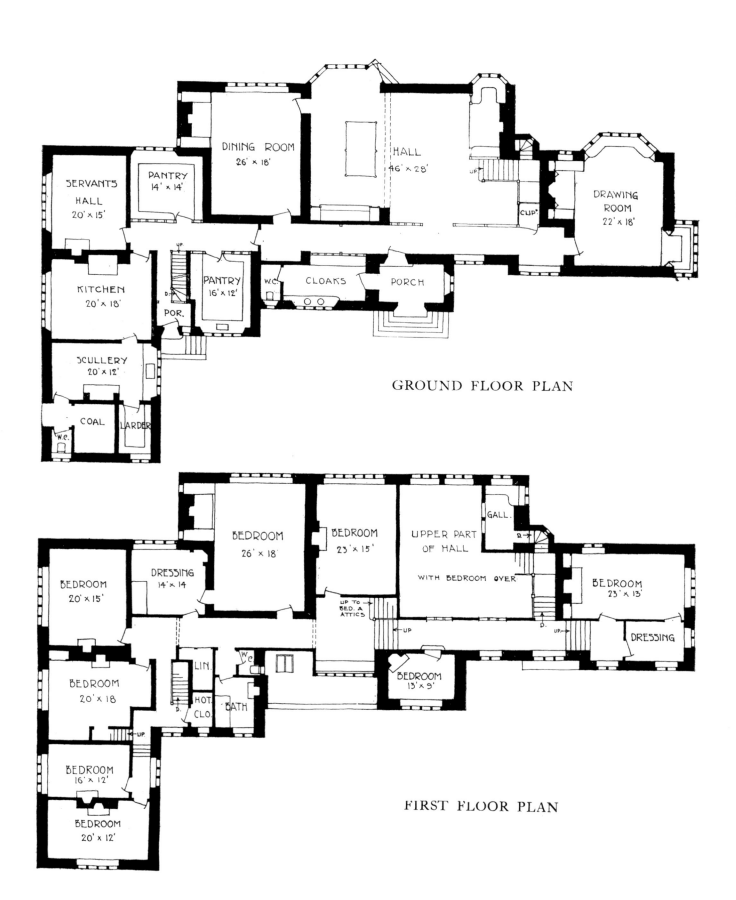

GROUND FLOOR PLAN

FIRST FLOOR PLAN

**Top:** Drawing of Blackwell made for Edward Holt, published in *The Studio*, 1901

**Opposite:** Blackwell ground and first floor plans published in *House & Garden*, 1906

## Mackay Hugh Baillie Scott
### Selected works

1892-93
The Red House, Victoria Road,
Douglas, Isle of Man

1897-98
Dining and drawing rooms (destroyed)
Ducal Palace, Darmstadt, Germany

1897-98
Village Hall, Onchan, Isle of Man

1898-99
Blackwell, Windermere,
Cumbria

1899-1901
Police Station, Castle Rushen,
Castletown, Isle of Man

1904-05
Elmwood Cottages, Letchworth
Hertfordshire

1907-11
Waldbühl, Uzwil, Switzerland

1908-09
Waterlow Court, Heath Close,
Hampstead Garden Suburb, London

1912-13
House, 48 Storey's Way, Cambridge

1924
Church, Rate Corner, Maltings Lane,
Cambridge

1928-9
Ashwood, Ashwood Road,
Woking, Surrey

Baillie Scott's first buildings were, to some extent, influenced by the great Arts & Crafts architects and designers of the day, principally Charles Francis Annesley Voysey (1857-1941), who designed Moor Crag and Broadleys by the shores of Windermere, not far from Blackwell. He would have seen Voysey's work in magazines such as *The Studio*, to which both men regularly contributed articles on architecture, and in which Baillie Scott's first article appeared in 1894.

His articles in *The Studio* magazine brought Baillie Scott to the attention of European clients, and in 1897 he was commissioned to create interior decorations and furnishings for the Grand Duke of Hesse's Palace at Darmstadt, Germany. This won the architect an international reputation and several more important commissions abroad. Baillie Scott was also engaged in the design of tapestries and furnishings for the Deutsche Werkstatten in Munich between 1900 and 1914.

Importantly, his next key commission after Darmstadt came from Edward Holt, for Blackwell. Drawings of a design for Blackwell were exhibited at the Royal Academy Summer Exhibition of 1898; however, it is possible they were made before he had visited the steep fellside site, as they were drawn on the flat, and without the familiar cylindrical Lakeland chimney pots that we can see at Blackwell today.

When Baillie Scott began work on Blackwell, the Scottish architect, Charles Rennie Mackintosh, who was three years his junior, was also forging a reputation. The Hill House at Helensburgh and several other of Mackintosh's designs show similarities with those of Baillie Scott. Both architects entered a German competition to design a *Haus eines Kunstfreundes* (House for an Art Lover) in 1901. No first prize was awarded, but Baillie Scott won second prize and Mackintosh, who had not complied with all the rules, was given a special prize. It is evident, when looking at his watercolours, that much of the inspiration for the interiors Baillie Scott submitted for the *Haus eines Kunstfreundes* competition came from Blackwell.

Baillie Scott was destined to make a major contribution to the already established Arts & Crafts Movement, which by the time he started work on Blackwell was already flourishing in the Lake District. John Ruskin, who had his home at Brantwood by Coniston Water, had done much to support the establishment of the Keswick School of Industrial Art in 1884 as well as the production of Langdale Linen and Ruskin Lace. Another outlet for the Arts & Crafts was Annie Garnett's Spinnery at

'A house may possess that inscrutable quality of the True Romance. Not shallow, showy and pretentious, as most modern mansions are, but full of still, quiet earnestness which seems to lull and soothe the spirit with promises of peace.'

M H Baillie Scott, 1906

**Above:** M H Baillie Scott designed oak chair, around 1895 and Manxman piano, around 1900
© Stuart Parker 2005

**Opposite:** Ground floor corridor to the White Drawing Room
© Clive Boursnell 2010

**Page 16:** Blackwell, Main Hall
© Nick Wood

Bowness. Mrs Holt visited the Spinnery in 1900 and her name appears in the visitors' book, though there appears to have been no record kept of what she might have bought.

As well as designing furniture as part of architectural commissions, Baillie Scott also developed a range of furniture that was made to his designs by the firm of J P White in Bedford, a well-established company used by other Arts & Crafts designers. His furniture was retailed directly by J P White, as well as through outlets such as Wylie and Lochhead in Glasgow and Liberty's of London. Baillie Scott's decision to move from the Isle of Man to Bedford in 1901 may well have been taken in order to supervise work on his range of furniture. The J P White Pyghtle Works catalogue of that year shows Baillie Scott furniture of striking originality and simplicity; it was avant-garde, taking inspiration from early British and European forms and transforming them for twentieth century life. Baillie Scott's popularity in Europe actually meant that J P White could open premises in Frankfurt and Dresden.

Baillie Scott is perhaps best known in Britain for his later cottage houses. He wanted to provide suitable alternative accommodation for his preferred clientèle, whom he described as *"...people with artistic aspirations but modest incomes..."* and, with this in mind, he opened up the room plan around a spacious living area. He continued to design more modest houses, mostly for the garden suburbs in southern England, until 1939 when, following the death of his wife, he closed his architectural practice.

In addition to Blackwell, Baillie Scott's long list of work includes fourteen houses in Cambridge, twelve houses on the Isle of Man, hotels and farms. Sadly, very few of his original architectural drawings or watercolours survive, as most were lost in two disastrous fires, one resulting from the bombing of his studio in the Second World War.

In 1945 Baillie Scott moved to a Brighton nursing home where he died on the 10th February, aged 79. He was survived by his son, also named Mackay Hugh Baillie Scott, and daughter, Enid Maud Mackay Hugh Baillie Scott. The epitaph carved on Baillie Scott's tombstone in Edenbridge Churchyard in Kent reads: *"Nature he loved, and Next to Nature, Art"*.

# House & Garden

Hermann Muthesius, an architect attached to the German Embassy in London between 1896 and 1903, included Blackwell in his influential 1904-5 book *Das Englische Haus* (*The English House*), which examined domestic architecture at the beginning of the twentieth century. He called it *"a most attractive creation in house-building"*.

Blackwell's location and orientation were key factors in its design; the house is perched on the hillside rather than down by the lake where already, by the 1890s, it was becoming almost suburban. The Lake District setting is further reinforced by the decorative detail inside, which takes the rowan tree, or mountain ash, as the unifying motif. Throughout the house wild flowers, berries and birds are found in the carvings, tiles, stained glass, and plaster work reflecting the natural environment outside.

Blackwell has a striking and impressive presence in the landscape. It is a grand statement, but Baillie Scott drew on elements of local vernacular architecture and reinterpreted them to his own purposes. Roughcast white-washed walls, steep pitched Westmorland slate roofs, cylindrical chimneys and multiple gables evoke Lakeland farmhouse architecture of the sixteenth and seventeenth centuries. Yet Baillie Scott's adaptation also produced an effect which is strikingly modern. Crisp sharp lines and minimal ornamentation create a complex orchestration of flat planes with sandstone window mullions set flush within the façades rather than being recessed as they would traditionally have been.

The house is beautifully integrated into the landscape, standing tall on the hillside with the White Drawing Room raised high, facing west and commanding wonderful views of Windermere and the Coniston fells beyond. Decorative elements are introduced on the outside of the building in the lead rainwater hoppers, some of which resemble castle turrets whilst others bear the initials of Edward Holt and the date, 1900, the planned date of Blackwell's completion. Holt's initials can also be seen in the original gates that have been re-hung on the fine slate piers topped with sandstone spheres. These mark the original, but now privately owned, driveway up to Blackwell.

Baillie Scott saw the gardens and terraces as yet another series of rooms flowing out from the main house, and they were critical in defining the setting of Blackwell on its fellside site. We know from records that

*"Blackwell is the most important surviving example of Baillie Scott's work in England."*

Martin Gayford, *Daily Telegraph*

**Above:** Azalias and Delphiniums, Blackwell's Garden Terraces

**Opposite:** Blackwell
© Lakeland Arts Trust

Thomas Mawson (1861-1933), the Windermere-based landscape designer, was involved in the design of the gardens. However, Baillie Scott may also have had some input as he had already worked on a number of garden designs. His most successful garden design was for Snowshill Manor in the Cotswolds in 1920, which is now owned by the National Trust and open to the public.

As this was only ever intended to be a holiday home, the gardens at Blackwell were quite simple and low maintenance, and, on the lower terrace, there were two lawn tennis courts. The series of terraces, arranged at different levels, are defined by substantial slate walls with giant buttresses. From each level the most important consideration was how to best experience the glorious views of the Lake District scenery.

The original plans for the gardens have not survived, although we can see the broad layout from early photographs. A new planting scheme has been implemented which is sympathetic to the architecture, whilst following the original principles of linking the house and garden with the surrounding landscape. The original planting scheme extended into the fields to the south of the house where several groups of trees and a small copse with rhododendrons were planted. This treatment creates the feeling that the whole of the Lake District is the garden, rather than a separate, defined area.

The modern planting scheme includes clematis, purple, red, pink and yellow tulips, crocus 'Citronella', dahlia 'David Howard', 'Johnson's Blue' geranium, 'Berkley Gold' iris, marigolds, alliums, cornflowers and fragrant herbs including lavender, sage and fennel. Rowan trees have also been planted as they provided the inspiration for much of the interior decoration.

# The Principal Rooms

Throughout Blackwell Baillie Scott used to the full the architectural elements of light, space, colour, different materials and decorative detailing, creating a very special architectural experience.

The glowing interiors combine exuberant plasterwork, intricate metalwork, stained glass, stonework, William de Morgan tiles and carved oak panelling. In almost every room different designs of daisies, bluebells, roses, rowan, hawthorn and oak are depicted. Little birds can also be seen weaving in and out of the carved wooden screens and capitals or fluttering their wings in the stained glass. Despite the richness of decorative detail, however, the effect is not fussy or cluttered. Each element is incorporated skilfully into the overall scheme to give a marvellously integrated and cohesive whole.

Baillie Scott was very skilful in his use of light inside the house and orientated Blackwell with the main rooms facing south, rather than west across the lake, so that the maximum benefit can be gained from sunlight throughout the day.

## The Main Hall

Baillie Scott was interested in challenging the tight planning of the typical Victorian house design to achieve a new open-plan spaciousness, and inside Blackwell the internal plan revolves around a large double-height hall. On entering the half-timbered Main Hall, one is taken back to medieval times. High above the oak panelling the eye is drawn to six stained glass windows, depicting the Holt family crest (showing two fleur-de-lys between two stylised rowan trees) and the institutions with whom the Holts were associated; Rugby School, Exeter and Christ Church Colleges, Oxford, Manchester City and Manchester University.

**Above:**   Delft tiles, the Main Hall fireplace

Leaf shaped door handle, Dining Room
© Charlotte Wood Photography

Carved oak ceiling boss in the Main Hall

**Opposite:** The Main Hall through to the Dinning Room
© Charlotte Wood Photography

As with a medieval hall, Blackwell's Main Hall would have been the principal entertaining area and a place for guests to gather and relax, and the space is made more fluid with the use of sliding doors. It also has a door opening onto the south lawn, allowing both physical and visual access to the gardens and the wider landscape beyond.

Playing billiards was a popular pursuit and Baillie Scott produced his own design for the six unusual dish-shaped beaten copper electric light shades that originally lit the billiard table. The light shades were re-hung after being discovered, forgotten, in a cupboard under the stairs soon after the Lakeland Arts Trust bought the house. It was not typical, in 1900, to give a billiard table such prominence and they were more commonly placed away from the central living area; however, this was a holiday home and the family would have used it somewhat differently - more informally - to their main family house.

Intimate areas were created in the inglenook, with settles set either side of a generous fireplace of huge interlocking blocks of local Ancaster stone and Broughton slate, and a lining of Delft tiles. These elements are echoed in the fireplace in the Dining Room, which is visible through the door opposite. A scaled-down corner version of this fireplace design has survived upstairs in what would have been the only en-suite bathroom. The blue and white Delft tiles are contemporary with Blackwell, despite the seventeenth century decorative motifs which further reinforce the baronial feel of the space.

Baillie Scott was in tune with the philosophy of John Ruskin, and throughout the house he incorporated Ruskin's belief that *"Good art flows from the craftsmen who create it"*. Furthermore, Baillie Scott was a designer who preferred to work with local craftspeople, and he positively encouraged them to draw out the qualities of their materials. The lower parts of the walls are clad in oak wainscot, with an intricate frieze of intertwined rowan berries, carved by Simpsons of Kendal.

Baillie Scott's furnishing designs were intended to complement his architecture and followed the same principles of fine craftsmanship with simple and elegant forms, offering an alternative to the overcrowded and fussy interiors that dominated the later nineteenth century. At Blackwell he also built in window or alcove seats in every room, which reduced the need for other furniture, allowing uninterrupted floor spaces.

One of the interesting pieces of furniture in the Main Hall is the 'Manxman' piano of around 1900, complete with a Broadwood movement, which was acquired for Blackwell by the Lakeland Arts Trust in 1999. Baillie Scott's design was cleverly disguised as an elegant, yet robust, cupboard with the keys hidden away behind doors decorated with horizontal strap-hinges. These hinges extend round the sides and end in a fleur-de-lys motif. The piano was intended to look good in any room, not just in a music room, and it sits perfectly in the oak panelled Main Hall. The Holt family were all musically trained and an early photograph (illustrated on p.9) shows a piano in the same position.

**Above:**  Shand Kydd (designed by W. Dennington), *Peacock Frieze* (detail), wallpaper, around 1905, the Main Hall

Carved oak panelling of rowan berry design (detail), by Simpsons of Kendal, Main Hall

Manxman piano, around 1900
© Stuart Parker

**Above:** Block printed and stencilled hessian wall covering, the Dining Room (detail), designed by Baillie Scott

Visitors today are encouraged to play the piano, and sheet music from the period is provided.

## The Peacock Frieze

The frieze in the Hall, which came from the popular Macclesfield wallpaper manufacturers Shand Kydd, has undergone careful conservation, which took nine months to complete. The 1905 photograph of the Hall in *Das Englische Haus* (illustrated on p. 9) shows the frieze to be absent, suggesting that it was a slightly later addition.

## The Minstrel's Gallery

This small room sits above the main fireplace, which in turn creates the cosy inglenook beneath. It provides an elevated space within the Main Hall, perched like a small tree house. From this viewpoint you can appreciate the true dimensions of the double-height hall. Earlier, in 1898, Baillie Scott had decorated and furnished a fantasy tree house, *'Le Nid'*, for the twenty-three-year-old Princess Marie of Romania, which does not survive.

His passion for all aspects of design, and his desire to create a unified whole, led Baillie Scott to design furniture and fabrics, such as the hessian wall covering in the Dining Room. He often gave his designs to craftspeople so that they could produce furniture and furnishings, and these were sold to the public through outlets such as Heal's and Liberty's.

## The Dining Room

Like the Main Hall, the Dining Room incorporates some strikingly modern elements for the period. The treatment of the fireplace is skilfully handled and the stained glass on either side of it is strongly Art Nouveau in its flowing organic lines.

Here, simple timber panelling acts as a foil to the main element of the room, the spectacular and extremely rare block-printed hessian wall covering. This has been painstakingly conserved, although the original blue background faded to brown a long time ago. Birds, daisies and harebells are represented in the bold design, as well as the decorative theme of rowan berries found throughout the house.

*'Blackwell was designed by an Arts & Crafts individualist of the first order… High on a hillside overlooking Windermere with the Coniston fells in the distance, it is a glorious location. Inside the rooms flow into each other… and the very female white drawing room, with delicate almost art-nouveau columns is alone worth the visit.'*

Hugh Pearman, *The Times*

Traditionally, family and guests would gather in the Drawing Room before being summoned for dinner by the butler. From here they would proceed through the hall to the dining room, warmed by a large fire. Dinner was taken at seven, and would always require formal dress. The butler, assisted by a maid, would serve several courses, and dinner would often last well into the evening. After dinner the ladies withdrew to the White Drawing Room for coffee, usually leaving the men to cigars, port and, perhaps, a game of billiards later.

## The White Drawing Room

The White Drawing Room at Blackwell is considered to be one of Baillie Scott's finest interiors. In stark contrast to the masculine feel of the Main Hall, this room is delightfully romantic and feminine. Here, again, are carvings of birds, leaves, roses, hawthorn berries and acorns. These natural forms create an almost Byzantine richness in the ceiling plasterwork, which survives miraculously intact. Every part of the space has been considered to make the most of the views and, in the early evening, golden sunlight floods into this room as the sun sets behind the Coniston fells.

The inglenook fireplace is the most complex and elegant in the house. It incorporates many different elements: stained glass, ceramic tiles, carved wooden capitals, alcoves, stonework, a mosaic floor, a pair of wonderful iron and enamelled fire dogs and a double mantel. The mantel shelf is not confined only to the fireplace, but metamorphoses into a shelf that could be used for the display of ceramics, which extends around the room, supported on slender columns. These tapering poles are topped with capitals of carved wood that branch out to reveal little birds, fruits and leaves. More birds dart between swaying tulips illuminated in the stained glass. Small mirrors set into the panelling give further brilliance to the light flooding in from the landscape that dances around the room throughout the day.

Finally, there is a beautifully restrained bay window affording magnificent views across Lake Windermere to the Coniston fells. Light not only falls from the sky, but is also reflected upwards from the lake onto the ceiling, bringing into sharp relief the intricate plasterwork. This window is positioned to be glimpsed from the main corridor and serves to create the dramatic crescendo of light which draws you along its length.

'…we seem already to have stepped into the world of fantasy and romance of the ancient bardic poetry that was once supposed to have been the legacy of the misty figure of Ossian… With Baillie Scott we are among the purely Northern poets among British architects.'

Hermann Muthesius (1867-1927)

## The Arts & Crafts Bedroom

There is no photographic evidence of how the Holts would have furnished the upstairs rooms, however it is clear from paint analysis that this bedroom would have been painted a golden yellow, as it is today. The bedroom and dressing room, as one of the principal suites, are situated above the White Drawing Room and enjoy spectacular views of the lake. As there was no adjoining bathroom there would be a washstand with a toilet set (jug, bowl, soap dish and toothbrush holder) for washing; it was part of the housemaid's duties to clean these each day and provide each bedroom with fresh water and linen. The original lights in these rooms did not survive, and have been replaced with pendant ceiling lights which date to around 1900 and a wall light designed by Baillie Scott.

## Corridors

The corridors are key architectural elements linking the principal rooms, both visually and in terms of access. In the ground floor corridor there are windows into the Main Hall as well as to the outside; the space flows from one area to another. The sliding doors are another clever device that totally alters the spatial relationships, depending on whether they are open or closed. Outside the White Drawing Room the passage widens, its panelling painted white, and carved columns are introduced in anticipation of the brilliant white room you are about to enter.

The upstairs landing is equally complex, with different levels of light provided by both external and internal windows and skylights. The levels change as you move along the landing and, at three different points, the corridor expands to break the rhythm and create deep bays, which almost become separate rooms in their own right.

## Colour

Colour plays a vital role in the interior decoration at Blackwell. Downstairs this is achieved largely by the combination of different materials, such as the warm rich tones of oak panelling, green slate set against pink sandstone, copper light fittings, and different coloured marbles to create vibrant mosaics. Baillie Scott researched in some depth the effect of colour on people's moods, and he often chose blue in the dining room for its calming qualities.

The upper floors once provided generous accommodation for the Holts and their five children, as well as for house guests. Paint analysis has revealed the colour schemes of the different rooms to be very bold - ranging from strong green to bright yellow. The colours of the walls related to those in the beautiful William de Morgan tiles gracing the fireplaces, as well as to those found in the stained glass windows.

The architect Roderick Gradidge writes about Blackwell in his book *Dream Houses: The Edwardian Ideal:*

*"For Baillie Scott there were three basic colour schemes. The first one was the dark colours that he used in dining rooms . . . The two other schemes relied on a great deal of white, most of Baillie Scott's furniture design being enamelled white or lightly stained an 'artistic' green. His pure white interiors often rely on a very sharp contrast of golden orange, perhaps combined with a pale blue or light purple and pink. It was these elegant, rather feminine colours that he considered suitable for drawing rooms. In bedrooms on the other hand he tended to use khaki greens, once again set off with intense patches of purple and pink. The palette is always very light and very clean, the watercolour washes seem almost to come straight from the tube without any mixing, and the contrast with the rather heavy colours of even such artistic designers of an earlier generation as William Morris and Norman Shaw is enormous."*

# Edwardian Life

Newly wealthy families, like the Holts, had no ancestral country seat so they commissioned architects to provide them with a house that would include elements of both country manor house and suburban villa. Tennis, rowing, sailing, music and billiards were the pastimes that Baillie Scott accommodated in his design. The Holts owned a steam launch, *Wasp*, which they kept in the boathouse on the lake.

Most importantly, the subtle planning of the house and gardens encouraged the Holts to lead a less formal life, opening out the living space and removing some of the rigid definitions common to nineteenth century interiors. The hall, far from being designed as an entrance space, took its inspiration from the medieval living hall, the hub of the home. It was a multi-purpose room, complete with billiard table, which anticipated the 'open plan' scheme popular today. Nothing could be further from the social conventions of the day than Baillie Scott's assertion that halls were a good place for children's play!

Blackwell was the perfect place for entertaining guests. A suite of guest rooms was included in the east wing of the house, and the Main Hall could accommodate a large gathering. The simple floor plan skilfully accommodated many of the elements demanded for correct social etiquette, with hall, dining room and drawing room fulfilling different roles.

The drawing room was primarily for the ladies of the house, for receiving female guests and discussions over afternoon tea. Often, on these occasions, the hostess made tea herself, serving guests from a spirit kettle. Evening gatherings where both sexes could meet informally were also held in the drawing room. Baillie Scott cleverly provided built-in seating for a relatively large gathering, as well as more intimate areas for private conversation.

## The Servants

Blackwell was designed to accommodate both the servants who lived in the house all year round and the servants that accompanied the Holts when they came to Blackwell from their main residence in Prestwich. The gardener and his family lived in one of Blackwell's lodges, and the Holts' chauffeur stayed at the other lodge when they came here. Nearly half of the floor space is dedicated to domestic staff and services, which helps to explain Blackwell's 'L' shape plan incorporating a service wing at the

**Above:**   Sailing boats on Windermere, around 1895

Steam Launch Branksome

Cyclists walking up Kendal Road in Bowness-on-Windermere, around 1900
Courtesy Kendal Library, Cumbria County Council

**Opposite:**   Joseph Holt pictured with the family dogs standing by the sundial, designed by Baillie Scott, which can still be seen today on the South Terrace, around 1905

east end of the house. The servants' hall and kitchens were placed at the front of the house so that staff could observe the entrance and the two driveways; the servants' hall is now the shop and reception, and the kitchen, where the fireplace that would have housed the cast-iron range still remains, is now the tearoom. These spaces were adapted in the 1940s for school and office use and, as a result, few original features have survived. Baillie Scott was concerned that servants were given rooms that were pleasant and well lit, and at Blackwell there was comparatively little difference between servants' and guest accommodation. The servants' rooms, in the second floor attics, are now the archive, library and offices.

Lady Holt was patroness of a home at Higher Broughton in Lancashire which trained motherless girls for domestic service, and it was from here that she selected her maids. The indoor servants led a regimented life and had little free time apart from Saturday evenings, when the family had high tea and a cold supper to allow the staff a few hours off. On Sundays attending church service at nearby Winster was compulsory for the servants and they walked the two miles each way.

The household's staff each had their own duties. Lady Holt would discuss the day's menus with the cook each morning. The parlourmaid, who was responsible for cleaning the silverware, also set the tables and carried in the family's meals. The in-between maid would clean the fireplaces and ground floor corridor and vestibule before breakfast and then assist the housemaid with her cleaning duties; all the cleaning was done using brushes as they did not have vacuum cleaners.

**Above:**    Issac Burrow, Blackwell's gardener

Maids from Storrs Hall hotel, Bowness-on-Windermere, in around 1900, dressed in the cap and 'fancy apron' worn for afternoon duties similar to that worn by Blackwell's maids.
Courtesy Kendal Library, Cumbria County Council

**Opposite:**  Blackwell
© Clive Boursnell 2010

# Recent History & Restoration

After the First World War, the Holts used Blackwell less and less and the house remained more or less empty apart from a skeleton staff of servants. The family made occasional visits, but seemed to have somewhat lost interest in Blackwell. This apparent lack of interest, however, is what has enabled Blackwell to survive so remarkably intact. Subsequent occupants of the building never actually owned it, and thus were not in a position to make significant alterations. The Holts also had little incentive to use their money on modernising a property that they leased out. As a consequence, most of the original features of Blackwell were thankfully still in place when it came to the notice of the Lakeland Arts Trust.

Blackwell was given a new lease of life during the Second World War, when pupils from Huyton College in Liverpool were evacuated there. One room on the first floor is named 'Miss Murphy's Room' in memory of the popular and forward thinking former Headmistress. After the war Blackwell continued as a school, finally closing in 1976. One of the garden terraces has been named in memory of the late Miss Jean McGowan, who taught at Blackwell for many years, and her companion, the late Miss Kay Dobie, who also worked at the school. Strong supporters of the Blackwell restoration project from the very beginning, they provided fascinating information about the history of the school as well as helping re-unite former pupils.

When the school closed, Blackwell was bought by a businessman who leased it as offices to the English Conservancy Council, later renamed English Nature. During their occupancy the decorative detail inside Blackwell was hidden from view behind boarded-up fireplaces and rows of filing cabinets. As a result, the delicate fittings were protected.

In 1997 English Nature moved out and the future of Blackwell was suddenly uncertain. Fearing that this great Arts & Crafts house, which at that time was only Grade II listed, could be irreparably damaged, the Lakeland Arts Trust stepped in. The Trust immediately approached the owner to buy the house even though, at that point, the building was not actually for sale and there were no funds for the purchase!

It was then a race against time to raise the money, first for the purchase, and then for the restoration of Blackwell. It was an enormous task and involved many difficult negotiations and a tremendous amount of hard

work. Bit by bit the pieces fell into place. Within ten months of starting the fund-raising campaign, the Trust had raised sufficient funds to buy Blackwell in February 1999. Further support from many private donors, charitable trusts and foundations, and a grant of £2.252 million from the Heritage Lottery Fund, enabled the Trust to proceed with Blackwell's full restoration.

This took just over a year and involved a great number of specialists in many different fields. The architects for the restoration were Allies and Morrison, led by Diane Haigh. The building refurbishment was carried out by restoration specialists William Anelay Ltd. In 2001 English Heritage raised Blackwell's listing status to the highest level of protection, Grade I. His Royal Highness The Prince of Wales supported the project from early on, visiting the house just before the restoration started, and, in September 2001, he visited Blackwell again to officially open the house to the public.

**Above:**     Repairing the roof in 2000
© Lakeland Arts Trust

Restoring the Peacock Frieze in 2000
© Lakeland Arts Trust

**Opposite:** Blackwell under wraps!
© Lakeland Arts Trust

Cleaning the panelling in the Main Hall.
The white band above the recess shows where
the Peacock Frieze had been removed for
conservation in 2000.
© Lakeland Arts Trust

*'Few rural galleries have the flair of Abbot Hall in the Lake District'*

Waldemar Januszczak *The Financial Times*

# The Lakeland Arts Trust

The Lakeland Arts Trust is a dynamic organisation creating opportunities for inspiration, understanding and enjoyment through the work of artists and craftspeople and the Trust's collections and buildings. The Trust runs Abbot Hall Art Gallery and the Museum of Lakeland Life and Industry in Kendal as well as Blackwell. The Windermere Steamboat Museum and Historic Boat Collection was transferred to the Trust in 2007.

Each of the Trust's facilities has its own characteristics, and provides a very special setting in which to see and enjoy art and history. Both Abbot Hall and Blackwell are Grade I listed buildings and were both rescued by the Trust. One hundred and fifty years apart in age, they offer very different environments: Abbot Hall is elegant and classical, whilst Blackwell is richly decorative and atmospheric. Abbot Hall Art Gallery has a national reputation for the collections of painting and sculpture and the exhibitions and events which bring national and international artists to Kendal. The historic ground floor rooms and light-filled galleries are an inspirational setting for the works. Recent exhibitions have included work by LS Lowry, RB Kitaj, Sheila Fell, Ben Nicholson, David Nash, Frank Auerbach, Stanley Spencer, Lucian Freud and Bridget Riley.

The Museum of Lakeland Life and Industry tells the story of the social and industrial past of the Lake District. Highlights of the Museum include reconstructed shops and rooms typical of the Victorian period and early 20th century, Arthur Ransome's illustrations and books, Arts and Crafts furniture by Simpsons of Kendal and historic photographs of the Lake District and its people.

The Trust holds regular exhibitions and events at Blackwell. The historic exhibitions and displays of contemporary craft, including ceramics, glass, textiles and silver, find a perfect setting in the house's decorative rooms. Talks and other events enable visitors to find out more about the Arts and Crafts Movement and contemporary craft. Contemporary craftspeople that have shown their work at Blackwell in the past few years include Philip Eglin, Edmund De Waal, Junko Mori, Jacqueline Ryan and David Roberts.

The Trust's wide-ranging learning programme aims to offer opportunities for all, from school visits to family workshops, lectures, walking tours and 'meet the artist' events.

In 2007 the Lakeland Arts Trust took over responsibility for the Windermere Steamboat Museum and Historic Boat Collection. All the boats in the collection were used on Lake Windermere and many of them were built locally. Most of the boats are of national significance including the steam launch SL Dolly (1850), believed to be the earliest working mechanically powered boat in the world, a collection of classic steam launches from the 1890s and 1900s, and experimental motor boats created between the 1920s and 1960s to compete for speed records on the lake. The Trust commenced the conservation programme in 2007 and is planning a capital programme to create a replacement museum where visitors will be able to see the boats on display, operating on the lake and being restored in the conservation workshop.

To find out more about the Lakeland Arts Trust visit our website www.lakelandartstrust.org.uk

**Above:**    S. L. Osprey, 1902

The boats are lifted from the Lake, 2000

Each boat has been assessed and given it's own conservation plan

**Opposite:**    J M W Turner (1775-1851)
*Windermere*, 1821
Given to Abbot Hall Art Gallery in 1999

**Above:**  Books with cover designs by Talwin Morris

**Opposite:**  Friend, Patrons and Benefactors Christmas
concert in the Main Hall at Blackwell
© Tony West Photography

## Study and Research

The Margaret Lawler Study Room includes many books on architecture, garden design, and the Arts & Crafts, as well as numerous other related books and periodicals. On long term loan from the Art Workers' Guild, there is also the library of specialist books that belonged to the architect and architectural historian Roderick Gradidge (1929-2000). Funds from the Aurelius Trust are helping us to purchase more books and periodicals for the collection.

The library is a wonderful resource, and is available for research purposes by appointment.

## Friends, Patrons & Benefactors

As an independent charity, Lakeland Arts Trust is dependent on the kindness of our donors, both through individual giving, and Charitable Trust donation. Our Friends, Patrons and Benefactors are vitally important in helping us look after the house and gardens at Blackwell, acquire and conserve important Arts & Crafts pieces, and ensure the continuation of high quality contemporary Arts & Crafts. Our Friends, Patrons and Benefactors enjoy a close relationship with us, receiving invitations to Private View evenings at Blackwell and Abbot Hall, advance notice of exhibitions and talks, and the opportunity to attend concerts and parties. If you feel inspired by our work, we would welcome your support. Please do approach us at Blackwell to discuss this, our contact details are listed within this publication.

## Legacy Gifts

More and more people are recognising the wonderful impact that a legacy gift can make. If you have found Blackwell inspirational, we ask that you consider making us a gift through your will. Your legacy will help ensure a long term future for the house and gardens at Blackwell, and support the acquisition and conservation of important Arts and Crafts pieces. If you would like more information about legacy giving, our Development Manager or Chief Executive would be pleased to discuss this in more detail. Information is also at www.lakelandartstrust.org.uk

# Acknowledgements

We are grateful for all the donations, grants and legacies that made Blackwell's restoration possible, and which have supported its care and development since.

Thomas Agnew Ltd
The Art Workers Guild - for long term loans to the collection
Aurelius Charitable Trust
AXA Provincial plc
Blackwall Green Ltd
Charlotte Bonham-Carter Charitable Trust
Crossfield Charitable Trust
Esmeé Fairbairn Foundation
The Hugh Fraser Foundation
Thomas Gibson Fine Art Ltd
The Gladstone Trust
The Goldsmiths' Company
The Hedley Foundation
Heritage Lottery Fund
Holt Charitable Trust
Idlewild Trust
JP Jacobs Charitable Trust - for the Muncaster Terrace
The Manifold Trust
The Monument Trust
The Henry Moore Foundation
The Moorhouse Charitable Trust
The Pilgrim Trust - for the restoration of the Dining Room
Philip Smith's Charitable Trust
Prince of Wales's Charitable Foundation
Garfield Weston Foundation

Sir Christopher and Lady Audland
In memory of Corinne Bennett - for the restoration of the fireside window stonework in the White Drawing Room
Dr Henry Mason Bibby
Claud Bicknell
John Borron
Mary E Burkett OBE
Lord and Lady Cavendish
Lord and Lady Chorley
Sir James Cropper KCVO
Kay Dobie and Jean McGowan - for the Herbaceous Terrace
John Entwistle
Dr Susan Evans

Oriole Goldsmith
Robert Hasell-McCosh
Lord Henderson of Brompton KCB
James Kirkman
Sir Mark Lennox-Boyd
In memory of Elsie and Mabel Longmire - for the Archive Room
Jocelyn Morton - for the Arts & Crafts Bedroom
Peter and Paddy Naylor and Adam and Marianne Naylor - for the restoration of the Peacock Frieze and Hall
Gillian Newbery
Jane Pollock
Nell Rhodes - for the Library in memory of Margaret Lawler and the restoration of the Minstrel's Gallery in memory of Isaac Rhodes
John and Pit Rink
Sir Oliver Scott Bt MD
Bernard Stanley
Oliver Thompson - for the Oliver Thompson Room
Brigadier & Mrs CE Tryon-Wilson
Dr Philip Welch - for the restoration of the wrought-iron work
Helen Williamson - for the restoration of the ground floor passageway oak panelling in memory of Marian Cowgill

In addition, there have been a number of anonymous donations as well as gifts for which we are extremely grateful.

We would like to thank the following for their assistance with the research of this guide: Dr Kathy Haslam, John Borron, Dr Jenni Brunton, Joan Bangor Jones and Huyton College Old Girls, Richard Kershaw, Simon Elliot, Diane Haigh, Peter Kelly, Gillian Riding, Simon Smith, Gavin Stamp, Tim Sturgis, Professor David Walker and Cherrie Trelogan.